PRINCEWILL LAGANG

Rise of the Creative Class: Artistry in Entrepreneurship

Contents

1

Rise of the Creative Class: Artistry in Entrepreneurship

Introduction

- Setting the Stage: Start with an engaging anecdote or statistics that highlight the increasing importance of creativity in the business world. Discuss the shift from the traditional industrial era to the knowledge-based economy.

- Thesis Statement: Introduce the central argument of the chapter, which is the rise of the creative class and its pivotal role in modern entrepreneurship.

Section 1: The Changing Landscape of Entrepreneurship

- The Entrepreneurial Ecosystem: Explore the evolution of the entrepreneurial landscape. Discuss the emergence of startups, innovation hubs, and the changing dynamics of business creation.

- The Knowledge Economy: Explain the shift from an industrial economy to a knowledge-based economy, where intellectual and creative resources are at a premium.

Section 2: The Creative Class Defined

- Defining the Creative Class: Discuss the characteristics and attributes of the creative class, which includes artists, designers, writers, and other creative professionals.

- Economic Significance: Highlight the economic significance of the creative class in terms of job creation, innovation, and economic growth.

Section 3: Creativity as a Competitive Advantage

- Creativity in Business: Explore the idea that creativity is a valuable asset for businesses, leading to product innovation, enhanced problem-solving, and a deeper connection with customers.

- Case Studies: Provide real-world examples of businesses and entrepreneurs who have leveraged creativity as a competitive advantage.

Section 4: Challenges and Opportunities

- Challenges Faced by the Creative Class: Discuss the obstacles and challenges that creative professionals often encounter in the business world, such as financial instability and the need for recognition.

- Opportunities for Creativity: Highlight the opportunities available to creative entrepreneurs, including the rise of the gig economy, freelance work, and the democratization of creative tools and platforms.

Section 5: Nurturing Creative Entrepreneurship

- Educational Initiatives: Explore the role of education and training in nurturing creative entrepreneurship. Discuss programs, courses, and initiatives that support creative professionals.

- Mentorship and Networking: Explain the importance of mentorship and networking for creative entrepreneurs, along with strategies for building a supportive community.

Section 6: The Road Ahead

- The Future of Creative Entrepreneurship: Speculate on the future of creative entrepreneurship in the ever-evolving business landscape. Discuss the potential for creative professionals to shape the future of work and commerce.

- Conclusion: Sum up the key points made in the chapter and reiterate the importance of the creative class in the world of entrepreneurship.

Chapter Summary

- Recap the Main Points: Provide a concise summary of the chapter's key takeaways and how they relate to the central thesis.

- Transition to Chapter 2: Offer a teaser or brief overview of what readers can expect in the next chapter, creating a seamless transition to the next part of the book.

—-

This chapter provides a comprehensive introduction to the rise of the creative class and its vital role in modern entrepreneurship. It sets the stage for the subsequent chapters that will delve deeper into the various aspects of creativity, innovation, and artistry in the world of business and entrepreneurship.

2

Cultivating Creativity: The Creative Mindset

Introduction

- Recap of Chapter 1: Briefly summarize the key points from Chapter 1, reminding readers of the rise of the creative class and its significance in entrepreneurship.

- Chapter 2 Overview: Introduce the focus of this chapter, which is the development of a creative mindset and the factors that influence it.

Section 1: The Creative Mindset

- What is a Creative Mindset?: Define the concept of a creative mindset, explaining how it differs from a traditional or linear mindset.

- Characteristics of a Creative Mindset: Explore the key characteristics and traits of individuals with a creative mindset, such as openness to new ideas, adaptability, and a willingness to take risks.

Section 2: Factors Shaping Creativity

- Genetics vs. Environment: Discuss the debate on whether creativity is primarily influenced by genetics or if it can be cultivated through environmental factors and experiences.

- Nurturing Creativity in Childhood: Examine the role of childhood experiences, education, and family support in shaping a creative mindset.

Section 3: Overcoming Creative Blocks

- Identifying Creative Blocks: Discuss common obstacles that creative individuals face, such as fear of failure, self-doubt, and burnout.

- Strategies for Overcoming Blocks: Offer practical strategies for overcoming creative blocks, including mindfulness, resilience, and self-compassion.

Section 4: Cultivating Creativity in the Workplace

- The Creative Organization: Explore the importance of fostering creativity in the workplace and how it contributes to innovation, problem-solving, and employee engagement.

- Leadership's Role: Discuss the role of leaders in creating an environment that encourages creative thinking and experimentation.

Section 5: Techniques for Enhancing Creativity

- Brainstorming and Idea Generation: Introduce techniques for generating creative ideas, including brainstorming, mind mapping, and ideation sessions.

- Mindfulness and Creativity: Explain how mindfulness practices can enhance creativity by promoting presence, focus, and divergent thinking.

Section 6: Case Studies

- Successful Creative Entrepreneurs: Showcase case studies of entrepreneurs who have harnessed a creative mindset to build successful businesses.

- Innovative Companies: Highlight companies known for their commitment to fostering creativity, such as Google, Apple, and IDEO.

Section 7: Cultivating Your Own Creative Mindset

- Practical Exercises: Provide readers with practical exercises and activities to help them develop and nurture their own creative mindset.

- Reflection and Journaling: Encourage readers to reflect on their own experiences and set goals for cultivating creativity.

Conclusion

- Summarize Key Points: Sum up the main takeaways from the chapter, emphasizing the importance of the creative mindset in entrepreneurship.

- Transition to Chapter 3: Provide a teaser or brief overview of what readers can expect in the next chapter, ensuring a smooth transition to the next part of the book.

—-

Chapter 2 explores the concept of the creative mindset and the various factors that influence it. It delves into the characteristics of a creative mindset, strategies for overcoming creative blocks, and techniques for enhancing creativity. Additionally, the chapter includes case studies and practical exercises to help readers cultivate their own creative mindset, preparing them for the challenges and opportunities of entrepreneurship in the creative age.

3

The Creative Process: From Idea to Innovation

Introduction

I - Recap of Previous Chapters: Provide a brief recap of the key concepts discussed in Chapter 1 and Chapter 2, emphasizing the importance of the creative class and the creative mindset.

- Chapter 3 Overview: Introduce the focus of this chapter, which is the creative process and how ideas evolve into innovations in the entrepreneurial context.

Section 1: Understanding the Creative Process

- What is the Creative Process?: Define the creative process and its stages, emphasizing that creativity is not a random act but a systematic and iterative endeavor.

- Stages of Creativity: Describe the various stages involved in the creative process, such as preparation, incubation, illumination, and verification.

Section 2: Ideation and Inspiration

- Idea Generation: Discuss techniques for generating and collecting ideas, such as brainstorming, mind mapping, and the use of inspiration sources.

- Creativity Sparks: Explore what sparks creativity and how to harness these moments of inspiration.

Section 3: Prototyping and Experimentation

- The Role of Prototyping: Explain the significance of prototyping in the creative process and how it allows for testing and refining ideas.

- Fostering a Culture of Experimentation: Discuss how entrepreneurs and organizations can create an environment that encourages experimentation and risk-taking.

Section 4: Innovation and Implementation

- Innovation Defined: Define innovation and its importance in the business world. Discuss how creative ideas are transformed into real-world innovations.

- Scaling and Commercialization: Explore the challenges and strategies for scaling and commercializing innovative products or services.

Section 5: Case Studies

- Innovative Entrepreneurs: Present case studies of entrepreneurs who have successfully navigated the creative process to develop groundbreaking innovations.

- Startup Success Stories: Highlight startups and companies that have leveraged the creative process to disrupt industries and achieve growth.

Section 6: Creativity and Problem Solving

- Problem Identification: Discuss how the creative process can be applied to problem-solving, helping entrepreneurs identify and address challenges.

- Design Thinking: Introduce the concept of design thinking and its role in finding innovative solutions.

Section 7: Challenges and Pitfalls

- Common Challenges in the Creative Process: Identify challenges and obstacles that entrepreneurs and creatives often face when navigating the creative process.

- Avoiding Creative Burnout: Discuss strategies for avoiding burnout and maintaining creativity throughout the process.

Conclusion

- Summarize Key Points: Sum up the main takeaways from the chapter, highlighting the importance of understanding and effectively applying the creative process in entrepreneurship.

- Transition to Chapter 4: Provide a teaser or brief overview of what readers can expect in the next chapter, ensuring a smooth transition to the next part of the book.

Chapter 3 delves into the creative process and how ideas evolve into innovations. It breaks down the stages of the creative process, explores ideation and inspiration techniques, and discusses the critical role of prototyping and experimentation. The chapter also includes case studies, practical insights into problem-solving, and a discussion of challenges and pitfalls faced during the creative process. By the end of this chapter, readers should have a solid understanding of how to take their creative ideas and turn them into innovative solutions within the entrepreneurial context.

4

Creativity in Business Models: Rethinking Entrepreneurial Strategies

I ntroduction

- Recap of Previous Chapters: Provide a brief recap of the key concepts discussed in Chapters 1, 2, and 3, emphasizing the importance of the creative class, the creative mindset, and the creative process.

- Chapter 4 Overview: Introduce the focus of this chapter, which is the integration of creativity into entrepreneurial strategies and business models.

Section 1: The Role of Creativity in Business Models

- Business Models Defined: Explain the concept of a business model and its importance in defining how an organization creates and delivers value.

- Creativity as a Competitive Advantage: Discuss how creativity can be a differentiator in developing innovative business models.

Section 2: Designing Innovative Business Models

- Business Model Canvas: Introduce the Business Model Canvas framework, which helps entrepreneurs visualize and innovate their business models.

- Components of a Business Model: Discuss the key components of a business model, such as customer segments, value proposition, channels, revenue streams, and cost structure.

Section 3: Value Innovation

- Value Innovation Defined: Explain the concept of value innovation, which involves simultaneously reducing costs and increasing value for customers.

- Blue Ocean Strategy: Discuss the Blue Ocean Strategy framework, which focuses on creating uncontested market space through value innovation.

Section 4: Sustainable and Impactful Business Models

- Sustainability in Business Models: Explore the role of sustainability and social impact in modern business models, discussing the triple bottom line approach.

- Impact Investing: Discuss impact investing and how it aligns with innovative business models that prioritize both profit and social or environmental good.

Section 5: Business Model Experimentation

- Lean Startup Methodology: Introduce the Lean Startup methodology and how it encourages entrepreneurs to iterate and experiment with their business models.

- Pivoting and Iterating: Discuss the concept of pivoting and why it's important for adapting and evolving business models.

Section 6: Case Studies

- Innovative Business Models: Present case studies of businesses and startups that have creatively redefined their business models to achieve success.

- Social Enterprises: Highlight social enterprises that have effectively combined creativity, innovation, and a social mission in their business models.

Section 7: Navigating Market Disruption

- Market Disruption: Discuss the concept of market disruption and how creative business models can be a response to industry upheaval.

- Examples of Market Disruption: Provide examples of industries that have been disrupted by innovative business models, such as the sharing economy and subscription services.

Conclusion

- Summarize Key Points: Sum up the main takeaways from the chapter, emphasizing the role of creativity in reshaping business models and strategies.

- Transition to Chapter 5: Provide a teaser or brief overview of what readers can expect in the next chapter, ensuring a smooth transition to the next part of the book.

—-

Chapter 4 focuses on the integration of creativity into business models and entrepreneurial strategies. It discusses the role of creativity in defining and rethinking business models, introduces frameworks like the Business Model Canvas and Blue Ocean Strategy, and explores the importance of sustainability and social impact in modern business models. The chapter also delves into the lean startup methodology, presents case studies of businesses with innovative models, and discusses how creative approaches can navigate market disruption. By the end of this chapter, readers should understand the power of creativity in redefining entrepreneurial strategies and achieving success in the competitive business landscape.

5

The Creative Entrepreneur's Toolkit: Skills, Resources, and Mindset

Introduction

- Recap of Previous Chapters: Provide a brief recap of the key concepts discussed in Chapters 1 through 4, emphasizing the importance of the creative class, the creative mindset, the creative process, and creative business models.

- Chapter 5 Overview: Introduce the focus of this chapter, which is the essential skills, resources, and mindset required for creative entrepreneurs.

Section 1: Essential Skills for Creative Entrepreneurs

- Creativity and Innovation Skills: Discuss the specific skills required for creative entrepreneurship, including problem-solving, adaptability, and the ability to think outside the box.

- Communication and Collaboration: Emphasize the importance of effective communication and collaboration skills in building partnerships and

17

attracting customers.

Section 2: Resourcefulness and Resilience

- Resourcefulness: Explain the concept of resourcefulness and how creative entrepreneurs often need to find creative solutions with limited resources.

- Resilience and Grit: Discuss the importance of resilience, grit, and the ability to persevere in the face of setbacks and failures.

Section 3: The Growth Mindset

- Growth Mindset Defined: Introduce the concept of the growth mindset, which involves a belief in the ability to develop skills and talents through effort and learning.

- Cultivating a Growth Mindset: Discuss strategies for cultivating a growth mindset, including embracing challenges and seeking continuous improvement.

Section 4: Emotional Intelligence

- Emotional Intelligence (EQ): Explain the importance of emotional intelligence in creative entrepreneurship, focusing on self-awareness, empathy, and relationship management.

- Managing Stress and Pressure: Discuss strategies for managing stress and pressure in high-stakes entrepreneurial situations.

Section 5: Financial Literacy

- Financial Management: Emphasize the importance of financial literacy and effective financial management in entrepreneurial ventures.

- Bootstrapping and Funding: Discuss bootstrapping strategies and various funding options available to creative entrepreneurs.

Section 6: Building a Support Network

- Mentorship and Networking: Highlight the value of mentorship and networking in creative entrepreneurship, offering guidance on how to build and leverage a support network.

- Online Communities and Resources: Discuss the role of online communities, forums, and resources that can connect creative entrepreneurs with like-minded individuals.

Section 7: Balancing Creativity and Business Acumen

- The Creative-Entrepreneur Balance: Explore the challenge of balancing artistic or creative pursuits with the business aspects of entrepreneurship.

- Finding Harmony: Discuss strategies for finding harmony between creative passion and financial success.

Conclusion

- Summarize Key Points: Sum up the main takeaways from the chapter, emphasizing the importance of developing the right skills, resources, and mindset for creative entrepreneurship.

- Transition to Chapter 6: Provide a teaser or brief overview of what readers can expect in the next chapter, ensuring a smooth transition to the next part of the book.

—-

Chapter 5 provides readers with the essential toolkit for creative entrepreneurship, including skills, resources, and the right mindset. It emphasizes the importance of creativity and innovation skills, resourcefulness, resilience, emotional intelligence, financial literacy, and building a support network. The chapter also addresses the challenge of balancing creativity with business acumen, preparing readers to navigate the entrepreneurial journey successfully. By the end of this chapter, readers should have a clear understanding of what it takes to thrive as a creative entrepreneur in today's business landscape.

6

From Concept to Market: Launching and Growing Your Creative Venture

Introduction

- Recap of Previous Chapters: Provide a brief recap of the key concepts discussed in Chapters 1 through 5, emphasizing the importance of the creative class, the creative mindset, the creative process, and the skills and resources required for creative entrepreneurship.

- Chapter 6 Overview: Introduce the focus of this chapter, which is the process of taking a creative concept or idea to market and growing a successful venture.

Section 1: Concept Development and Validation

- Concept to Reality: Discuss the transition from a creative idea to a viable concept for a product or service.

- Market Research and Validation: Explain the importance of market research and validation to ensure there is a demand for the product or service.

Section 2: Business Planning and Strategy

- Business Plan: Discuss the development of a comprehensive business plan, covering areas such as business model, financial projections, and marketing strategy.

- Strategic Planning: Emphasize the need for strategic planning, setting short-term and long-term goals, and adapting to changing market conditions.

Section 3: Branding and Marketing

- Branding: Discuss the significance of branding and how it conveys the essence of the venture to customers.

- Marketing Strategy: Explore various marketing strategies, including digital marketing, content marketing, and influencer partnerships.

Section 4: Product Development and Innovation

- Product Development Process: Explain the stages involved in developing and refining a product or service, emphasizing the importance of continuous innovation.

- User-Centered Design: Discuss the value of user-centered design and involving customers in the development process.

Section 5: Sales and Distribution

- Sales Strategies: Discuss different sales strategies, from direct sales to partnerships and e-commerce.

- Distribution Channels: Explore options for distribution, including traditional retail, e-commerce platforms, and third-party distributors.

Section 6: Financial Management and Scaling

- Financial Management: Discuss the ongoing financial management of the venture, including budgeting, cash flow management, and scaling the business.

- Growth Strategies: Explore various growth strategies, such as expanding to new markets, diversifying product lines, and securing additional funding.

Section 7: Challenges and Adaptation

- Challenges in Entrepreneurship: Identify common challenges faced by entrepreneurs and how to adapt and pivot when necessary.

- Learning from Failure: Discuss the importance of learning from failure and using setbacks as opportunities for growth.

Conclusion

- Summarize Key Points: Sum up the main takeaways from the chapter, emphasizing the process of launching and growing a creative venture.

- Transition to Chapter 7: Provide a teaser or brief overview of what readers can expect in the next chapter, ensuring a smooth transition to the next part of the book.

—-

Chapter 6 guides readers through the journey of taking a creative concept to market and growing a successful venture. It covers concept development, business planning, branding, marketing, product development, sales, distribution, financial management, and the challenges entrepreneurs may face along the way. By the end of this chapter, readers should have a solid understanding of the practical steps and strategies needed to launch and grow a creative business successfully in a competitive market.

7

Sustaining Creativity: Navigating Challenges and Staying Innovative

I ntroduction

- Recap of Previous Chapters: Provide a brief recap of the key concepts discussed in Chapters 1 through 6, emphasizing the importance of the creative class, the creative mindset, the creative process, the skills and resources required, and the process of launching and growing a creative venture.

- Chapter 7 Overview: Introduce the focus of this chapter, which is the sustainability of creativity in entrepreneurship, overcoming challenges, and maintaining innovation.

Section 1: The Creative Entrepreneur's Mindset

- Resilience and Adaptability: Discuss the importance of a resilient and adaptable mindset for creative entrepreneurs, as they face unforeseen challenges and changes.

- Staying Curious: Emphasize the value of curiosity and a hunger for learning to maintain innovation.

Section 2: Innovation in a Changing Landscape

- Continuous Innovation: Discuss the need for constant innovation to stay competitive and relevant in a dynamic business environment.

- Market Trends and Technology: Explore how staying up-to-date with market trends and emerging technologies can drive innovation.

Section 3: Navigating Market Competition

- Understanding Market Competition: Explain the significance of understanding and monitoring competitors in the market.

- Differentiation Strategies: Discuss strategies for differentiation and carving out a unique market position.

Section 4: Managing Growth and Scaling

- Scaling Challenges: Address the challenges associated with scaling a creative venture, including maintaining quality and culture.

- Scaling Strategies: Explore various strategies for successful scaling, such as strategic partnerships and expansion into new markets.

Section 5: Leadership and Team Development

- Effective Leadership: Discuss the role of effective leadership in sustaining creativity, managing teams, and fostering a culture of innovation.

- Team Development: Emphasize the importance of team development, including hiring, training, and mentoring creative talent.

Section 6: Adapting to Industry Disruption

- Anticipating Disruption: Discuss the need to anticipate and adapt to industry disruptions to remain competitive.

- Pivoting and Innovation: Explore how innovation and pivoting can be a response to industry challenges.

Section 7: Sustainability and Social Responsibility

- Sustainability Initiatives: Discuss the role of sustainability and corporate social responsibility in sustaining creativity and appealing to conscious consumers.

- Environmental and Social Impact: Explore the impact of business decisions on the environment and society.

Conclusion

- Summarize Key Points: Sum up the main takeaways from the chapter, emphasizing the importance of sustaining creativity, adapting to change, and staying innovative in entrepreneurship.

- Transition to the Conclusion: Provide a brief overview of what readers can expect in the book's conclusion, offering a final perspective on the journey of creative entrepreneurship.

—-

Chapter 7 addresses the critical aspects of sustaining creativity in the entrepreneurial journey, including maintaining the right mindset, continuous innovation, navigating market competition, managing growth and scaling, effective leadership, adapting to industry disruption, and embracing sustainability and social responsibility. By the end of this chapter, readers should have a comprehensive understanding of how to overcome challenges and maintain their creative edge while building and growing their entrepreneurial ventures.

8

The Future of Creative Entrepreneurship: Trends and Opportunities

Introduction

- Recap of Previous Chapters: Provide a brief recap of the key concepts discussed in Chapters 1 through 7, emphasizing the importance of the creative class, the creative mindset, the creative process, the skills and resources required, the process of launching and growing a creative venture, and sustaining creativity.

- Chapter 8 Overview: Introduce the focus of this chapter, which is the exploration of future trends and opportunities in the field of creative entrepreneurship.

Section 1: Emerging Technologies and Innovation

- Technology-Driven Innovation: Discuss the impact of emerging technologies such as AI, blockchain, and virtual reality on creative entrepreneurship.

- Opportunities for Tech Integration: Explore how creative entrepreneurs can harness these technologies to create new products and services.

Section 2: Creative Collaborations and Cross-Disciplinary Work

- Collaboration Trends: Discuss the rising trend of creative collaborations between artists, designers, and entrepreneurs in different disciplines.

- Cross-Disciplinary Opportunities: Explore the opportunities for cross-disciplinary work that can lead to innovation and unique creative ventures.

Section 3: Sustainability and Social Impact

- Sustainability as a Necessity: Explain how sustainability is no longer an option but a necessity for creative ventures, and how it can drive innovation.

- Social Entrepreneurship: Explore the growing field of social entrepreneurship and how creative entrepreneurs can create positive impact alongside profit.

Section 4: Niche Markets and Personalization

- The Power of Niche Markets: Discuss the value of targeting niche markets and serving specific customer segments.

- Personalization Strategies: Explore personalization trends and the use of data to cater to individual preferences.

Section 5: Cultural and Global Opportunities

- Cultural Relevance: Discuss the importance of cultural relevance and how it can be leveraged in creative entrepreneurship.

- Global Expansion: Explore opportunities for expanding creative ventures to international markets and the challenges associated with global business.

Section 6: Ethical Entrepreneurship

- Ethical Business Practices: Discuss the rise of ethical entrepreneurship, focusing on transparency, fair labor practices, and responsible sourcing.

- Consumer Values: Explore how consumer values and ethics are shaping the creative entrepreneurship landscape.

Section 7: Preparing for the Future

- Adaptation and Continuous Learning: Discuss the importance of adaptation and continuous learning to stay ahead in the ever-evolving field of creative entrepreneurship.

- Investing in Creativity: Explore strategies for investing in creativity and innovation to future-proof a creative venture.

Conclusion

- Summarize Key Points: Sum up the main takeaways from the chapter, emphasizing the future trends and opportunities in creative entrepreneurship.

- Transition to the Conclusion: Provide a final perspective on the future of creative entrepreneurship, reiterating the book's central themes and the potential for creativity in entrepreneurship.

—-

Chapter 8 offers readers insights into the future of creative entrepreneurship, highlighting emerging trends and opportunities. It covers the impact of technology, creative collaborations, sustainability, personalization, cultural and global considerations, ethical entrepreneurship, and the importance of adaptation and continuous learning. By the end of this chapter, readers should have a forward-looking perspective on how to position themselves for success in the dynamic landscape of creative entrepreneurship.

9

The Creative Entrepreneur's Legacy: Impact and Inspiration

Introduction

- Recap of Previous Chapters: Provide a brief recap of the key concepts discussed in Chapters 1 through 8, emphasizing the journey of creative entrepreneurship, the challenges and opportunities, and the future trends.

- Chapter 9 Overview: Introduce the focus of this chapter, which is the idea of leaving a lasting legacy as a creative entrepreneur and inspiring future generations.

Section 1: The Legacy of Creative Entrepreneurs

- Defining Legacy: Discuss what it means to leave a legacy as a creative entrepreneur and why it matters.

- Examples of Legacy: Highlight examples of creative entrepreneurs who have left a lasting impact on their industries and communities.

Section 2: Social Impact and Responsibility

- Social Responsibility: Explore the role of creative entrepreneurs in giving back to society and contributing to positive social change.

- Philanthropy and Impact Initiatives: Discuss ways in which creative entrepreneurs can establish philanthropic endeavors and impact initiatives.

Section 3: Mentorship and Education

- Mentorship Programs: Discuss the importance of mentorship in the creative entrepreneurship ecosystem and how experienced entrepreneurs can guide the next generation.

- Educational Initiatives: Explore the establishment of educational programs and initiatives that promote creativity and entrepreneurship.

Section 4: Inspiring the Next Generation

- Inspiring Future Entrepreneurs: Discuss strategies for inspiring and motivating the next generation of creative entrepreneurs.

- Sharing Experiences: Share personal stories and insights from successful creative entrepreneurs that can serve as inspiration.

Section 5: Documenting and Preserving Creativity

- Archiving Creative Work: Discuss the importance of documenting and preserving creative work, including art, products, and ideas.

- Cultural and Historical Significance: Explore how creative entrepreneurship contributes to culture and history.

Section 6: The Cycle of Creativity

- The Creative Ecosystem: Explain how creative entrepreneurship is part of a larger ecosystem that supports and sustains creativity.

- The Cycle of Innovation: Explore how innovation and creativity continue to evolve and inspire new generations.

Conclusion

- Summarize Key Points: Sum up the main takeaways from the chapter, emphasizing the importance of leaving a legacy, making a positive impact, and inspiring others as a creative entrepreneur.

- Final Thoughts: Provide a concluding message on the significance of creativity, innovation, and entrepreneurship in shaping a better future.

—-

Chapter 9 focuses on the concept of leaving a legacy as a creative entrepreneur and inspiring future generations. It discusses the legacy of creative entrepreneurs, the importance of social impact and responsibility, mentorship and education, and strategies for inspiring the next generation. The chapter also touches on the preservation of creativity and its role in culture and history. By the end of this chapter, readers should have a profound understanding of the lasting impact creative entrepreneurship can have on society and the potential to inspire positive change.

10

The Creative Entrepreneur's Journey: Reflections and Future Directions

I ntroduction

- Recap of the Book: Provide a brief recap of the key concepts discussed throughout the book, summarizing the journey of creative entrepreneurship, challenges, opportunities, and the legacy of creative entrepreneurs.

- Chapter 10 Overview: Introduce the focus of this final chapter, which is a reflection on the creative entrepreneur's journey and a glimpse into the future of creative entrepreneurship.

Section 1: Reflections on the Entrepreneurial Journey

- Personal Growth and Development: Discuss the personal growth and development experienced by creative entrepreneurs during their journey.

- Successes and Failures: Reflect on the successes and failures that have shaped their path.

Section 2: The Impact of Creative Entrepreneurship

- Societal and Economic Impact: Discuss the broader impact of creative entrepreneurship on society and the economy.

- Case Studies of Impact: Share case studies of creative entrepreneurs who have made a significant impact.

Section 3: Lessons Learned and Key Takeaways

- Key Lessons: Summarize the key lessons learned throughout the book, emphasizing the importance of creativity, innovation, and adaptability.

- Practical Insights: Offer practical insights and advice for aspiring creative entrepreneurs based on the book's content.

Section 4: Future Directions in Creative Entrepreneurship

- Emerging Trends: Discuss the emerging trends in creative entrepreneurship and the future landscape of business.

- Opportunities and Challenges: Explore the opportunities and challenges that the next generation of creative entrepreneurs may face.

Section 5: The Creative Entrepreneur's Ongoing Role

- Advocacy and Mentorship: Discuss the role of established creative entrepreneurs in advocacy and mentorship.

- Continuing Innovation: Emphasize the importance of ongoing innovation and adaptation for creative entrepreneurs.

Conclusion

- Final Reflections: Sum up the main themes and insights from the book, highlighting the significance of creative entrepreneurship in today's world.

- The Ongoing Journey: Offer a final message on the continued journey of creative entrepreneurship and the potential for creating positive change through creativity and innovation.

—-

Chapter 10 serves as the concluding chapter of the book, offering reflections on the creative entrepreneur's journey, insights into the impact of creative entrepreneurship, and the key lessons and takeaways from the book. It also provides a glimpse into the future of creative entrepreneurship, highlighting emerging trends and the ongoing role of creative entrepreneurs in shaping the business landscape. By the end of this chapter, readers should leave with a sense of inspiration, reflection, and a vision for their own creative entrepreneurial journey.

11

Summary

Title: "Rise of the Creative Class: Artistry in Entrepreneurship"

Chapter 1: Rise of the Creative Class: Artistry in Entrepreneurship
- This chapter sets the stage for the book by introducing the rise of the creative class and its significance in the world of entrepreneurship. It explores how creativity and artistry have become essential in the modern business landscape, driving innovation and economic growth.

Chapter 2: Cultivating Creativity: The Creative Mindset
- Chapter 2 delves into the concept of the creative mindset, exploring its characteristics and traits. It discusses the factors that shape creativity, offers strategies for overcoming creative blocks, and highlights techniques for enhancing creativity in the workplace.

Chapter 3: The Creative Process: From Idea to Innovation
- In Chapter 3, the creative process is the focus. It breaks down the stages of the creative process, from idea generation to innovation, and provides insights into ideation, prototyping, and problem-solving. Case studies illustrate how entrepreneurs have successfully navigated this process.

Chapter 4: Creativity in Business Models: Rethinking Entrepreneurial

Strategies

- Chapter 4 discusses the integration of creativity into business models and entrepreneurial strategies. It covers the Business Model Canvas, value innovation, sustainability, and practical insights for scaling and redefining business models.

Chapter 5: The Creative Entrepreneur's Toolkit: Skills, Resources, and Mindset

- Chapter 5 provides readers with the essential toolkit for creative entrepreneurship, including skills, resources, and mindset. It emphasizes the importance of creativity and innovation skills, resourcefulness, resilience, and the growth mindset.

Chapter 6: From Concept to Market: Launching and Growing Your Creative Venture

- Chapter 6 guides readers through the journey of taking a creative concept to market and growing a successful venture. It covers concept development, business planning, branding, marketing, product development, sales, distribution, financial management, and scaling.

Chapter 7: Sustaining Creativity: Navigating Challenges and Staying Innovative

- Chapter 7 addresses the critical aspects of sustaining creativity in the entrepreneurial journey, including maintaining the right mindset, continuous innovation, navigating market competition, and embracing sustainability and social responsibility.

Chapter 8: The Future of Creative Entrepreneurship: Trends and Opportunities

- In Chapter 8, readers gain insights into the future of creative entrepreneurship, highlighting emerging trends in technology, cross-disciplinary work, sustainability, personalization, and more. The chapter explores how creative entrepreneurs can position themselves for success in a dynamic landscape.

Chapter 9: The Creative Entrepreneur's Legacy: Impact and Inspiration

- Chapter 9 focuses on leaving a legacy as a creative entrepreneur and inspiring future generations. It discusses social impact and responsibility, mentorship, and the preservation of creativity. The goal is to inspire positive change through creative entrepreneurship.

Chapter 10: The Creative Entrepreneur's Journey: Reflections and Future Directions

- Chapter 10 offers reflections on the creative entrepreneur's journey, insights into the impact of creative entrepreneurship, key lessons, and a glimpse into future trends. It concludes by emphasizing the ongoing journey of creativity and innovation.

This book provides a comprehensive guide for creative entrepreneurs, from understanding the creative mindset and process to launching, growing, and sustaining their ventures. It also explores future trends and opportunities, the importance of leaving a legacy, and the ongoing cycle of creativity and innovation.